The Best Poems of
JOHN BANISTER TABB

The Best Poems

OF

JOHN BANISTER TABB

edited with an introduction

By FRANCIS E. LITZ

Professor of English
Catholic University of America

THE NEWMAN PRESS
Westminster, Maryland
1957

Copyright © 1957 by THE NEWMAN PRESS
Library of Congress Catalog Card Number: 57-11823
Printed in the United States of America

O little bird,

I'd be like thee,

Singing my native song—

Brief to the ear

But long to love and memory.

CONTENTS

INTRODUCTION

FATHER JOHN BANISTER TABB was born on March 22, 1845, at "The Forest" in Amelia County, Virginia. His early life on the family plantation was the seed-time of his poetry and his first contacts with the world of nature and man were pleasant and ennobling. The hills, streams, birds, flowers, trees, and wind, as he said, "my kinsmen all were they." Among the later poems that had their origin here are "Killdee" (28),* "The Lonely Mountain" (32), "The Humming-Bird" (52), "The Cowslip" (155), and "The Whip-poor-will" (204).

The pleasures of life on an ante-bellum plantation were his until the late summer of 1862, when he left home—and a South he was never again to know—to serve as a blockade-runner. Captured on June 4, 1864, off Beaufort, North Carolina, by the federal *Keystone State*, he spent the next seven months as a prisoner of war at Bull Pen, Point Lookout, Maryland, where he met Sidney Lanier. The two became fast friends, and Father Tabb later expressed his devotion to Lanier in a number of poems (67, 94).

* The figures in parentheses are the numbers assigned to the poems in this collection.

Returning home from the prison-camp, young Tabb found his family and their estate ruined. In his desire to aid them he went to Baltimore to prepare himself for a career as a pianist, but a year afterwards he was forced to abandon it because his benefactor could no longer support him. Then he turned to teaching and to the ministry. He taught at St. Paul's School for Boys in Baltimore and presented himself as a candidate for orders in the Episcopal Church. Although he soon accepted a position at Racine College, he was called home shortly after his arrival because his sister Hallie was ill. Religious doubts were also disturbing him. He stayed at home, assisting his family as best he could and battling through his spiritual crisis until, like his friend William Curtis, he decided to become a Catholic and to study for the priesthood.

The two years, 1870–1872, must have been extremely difficult, for the Tabbs had been Anglicans before they came to Virginia in 1637, and they made him keenly aware of their disapproval. In fact, he was to know little else but mental anguish during the 70's. Poverty was crushing the South and it did not spare his family, once among the wealthiest. When John Tabb entered St. Charles College in November, 1872, he walked the five and a half miles from Ellicott City, Maryland, and carried all his possessions, other than the suit he wore, in a small handbag.

After his graduation in 1875, because of the financial needs of his family, he did not go to the Seminary. He taught at St. Peter's School in Richmond from 1875 to 1877, at the same time probably assisting the then Bishop Gibbons with the writing of *The Faith of Our*

Fathers, and teaching later at St. Charles College from 1877 to 1881. Only in the latter year did he commence his theological studies at St. Mary's Seminary, Baltimore. Immediately after his ordination, December 20, 1884, he returned to St. Charles to resume his double career of teaching aspirants to the priesthood and of writing poetry. He might have lived as a secular priest in some rural parish and given his leisure hours to the Muses as did his prototype Robert Herrick in seventeenth-century England; but, because he loved teaching, he chose to remain at St. Charles.

Few teachers ever succeeded in leaving as indelible impressions upon their students as he, who, without any formal training in the art of teaching, was himself the teacher supreme. Somehow he established an intimate contact with the minds of all before him and his great soul communicated directly with theirs, opening visions of beauty through imagery and rhythm: the Skylark—cloud of fire, star of heaven, blithe spirit, pouring forth its full heart in profuse strains of unpremeditated art; the Nightingale—not born for death, whose voice was heard in ancient days; the Ancient Mariner—alone on a wide, wide sea; the Lady of Shalott—lying robed in snowy white; and many other famous characters and scenes, the ghosts of which still linger in his favorite quotations preserved in that unique book of his—*Bone Rules, or Skeleton of English Grammar*—which he used in his classes as a point of departure. But his wit and humor were always on tap to relieve and stimulate—through anecdote, quip, pun or impromptu limerick. A phrase in a story he was reading or in a poem he was reciting, a student's comment or answer, an incident of the class period were all likely to touch off a merry mood,

In his teaching Father Tabb also exercised his priesthood. Always he kept before his own mind and before the minds of his students the ideals of the priestly life and stressed the virtues of the sacerdotal calling. If his priestly ministrations were limited by the kind of life he led at the College, his priestly character, however, pervaded his poetry just as it did his teaching. The imagery of his poems reveals how deeply Catholic doctrine and practice had penetrated his spiritual nature and artistic imagination. He had the same sensibility to flowers and birds as Wordsworth, the same rapturous contemplation of the cloud and lark as Shelley; but he expressed these experiences in religious symbols. A fundamental difference between him and Emily Dickinson, with whom he has often been compared, is that he accepts Christianity and the Catholic Church in his poems and she holds the vaguest sort of belief and professes no orthodox religion. Perhaps it is this liberalism that makes the New England poet more attractive to the contemporary literary man than the priest-poet. Old Testament history, New Testaments parables, the liturgy, the sacraments, theological dogma, hagiography furnish the symbols for Tabb's interpretation of the world of nature and man (10, 13, 14, 37, 53, 74, 80, 97, 99, 107, 121, 151, 168, 174, 179, 183, 188, 208, 212, 241, 248). He judges the thought and action of human beings according to Christian morality. He looks upon life with the mind of Christ.

When Father Tabb took up his permanent residence at St. Charles in 1884, he found himself in one of the most delightful sections of Maryland—Howard County— the foothills of the Alleghanies, through which until recently curved the Old Frederick Pike, rolling country made picturesque by cultivated fields, rich woodlands, and winding streams. He began to enjoy peace of mind and security and had the opportunity of exploring every nook and corner of Howard County. In such a lovely region he, like Wordsworth, "had forms distinct to steady him, and his body could drink in a restoration like the calm of sleep." Nature began to absorb his observations, and what he saw and heard brightened his outlook on life and his poetry. One of the earliest poems written after his return, in the spring of 1885, is "The Water-Lily," a charming, lilting fancy, identifying the water-lily as the garment left in the tide by the maiden moon (24). A more serious note is struck in "Fraternity," which Professor Mather suggested ought to be called rather "Predestination unto Poetry":

> I know not but in every leaf
>   That sprang to life along with me
> Were written all the joy and grief
>   Thenceforth my fate to be.
>
> The wind that whispered to the earth,
>   The bird that sang its earliest lay,
> The flower that blossomed at my birth—
>   My kinsmen all were they.
>
> Aye, but for fellowship with these
>   I had not been—nay, might not be;
> Nor they but vagrant melodies
>   Till harmonized to me.

Humor, too, found its way into his poems of nature and verses for children, such as these:

JACK FROST'S APOLOGY

To strip you of your foliage
My spirit sorely grieves;
Nor will I in the work engage
Unless you grant your leaves.

THE TAX-GATHERER

"And pray, who are you?"
Said the violet blue
To the Bee, with surprise
At his wonderful size,
In her eye-glass of dew.
"I, Madam," quoth he,
"Am a publican Bee,
Collecting the tax
On honey and wax;
Have you nothing for me?"

Four-fifths of all his poems were written at old St. Charles College. He was more familiar with the country about him than any other person there. Sometimes he chose a student to accompany him on his jaunts, but more frequently he went alone. His favorite walks were to Doughregan Manor—the home of the Carrolls, the Old Mill, and Folly Quarters. Many of his poems had their origin, even their finished form, during these "pilgrimages." Instances of these precious experiences are recorded in "Cherry Bloom" (131), "Wood Grain" (205), "Clover" (123), "Wild Flowers" (107), "Mignonette" (126), "Exaltation" (140), and "Dandelion" (72).

Father Tabb lived at St. Charles College the rest of his life. Only his summers were spent elsewhere. From the closing of the College until its opening in September, he remained with his sister Hallie in a small house on the old estate, which he himself in 1895 called the "loneliest spot in America." During these years he published An Octave to Mary (1893), Poems (1894), Lyrics (1897), Child Verse (1899), Two Lyrics (1900), Later Lyrics (1902), The Rosary in Rhyme (1904), Quips and Quiddits (1907), and Later Poems (1910). Other poems which were uncollected or previously unpublished can be found in my biography, Father Tabb— A Study of His Life and Works (The Johns Hopkins Press). The poet-priest has also left a personal record of the years he spent at the College, as well as those before 1884, in the letters he wrote to friends and the articles that appeared in The Independent.*

The spirituality inspiring Father Tabb's poetry was never more in evidence than when total blindness, which had threatened him for many years, descended upon him in 1908. The thoughts and feelings prompted by this affliction are recorded in "A Sunset Song" (235), "Going Blind" (236), "In Blindness" (237), "Waves" (240), "Blind" (242), "The Smiter" (243), "Mammy" (247), and "Fiat Lux" (248). Death came in the way he had wished in the early sonnet "Unmoored" (8), during the night of November 19, 1909. His body lies buried in Gordon Blair's plot in Hollywood Cemetery, Richmond, Virginia.

Father Tabb deserves to be considered an experimenter in poetry, like Whitman, Lanier, and Dickinson, as an examination of his poems, particularly those written between 1884 and 1894, will show. First, he was per-

* See Father Tabb's Letters—Grave and Gay and Other Prose, ed. F. E. Litz, Washington, D.C.: Catholic University Press, 1950.

haps the earliest of the pre-Eliot poets to write in the metaphysical manner; and, secondly, he was obviously doing in his way what Hopkins and Dickinson were also doing—using a special syntactical approach to achieve a form of extraordinary compression. It should be remembered that his poems were known by the reading public before Emily Dickinson's; nor did he know hers until 1894.

Father Tabb's early lyric and narrative efforts, echoing Lanier, Hood, Shelley, Poe, and Tennyson, and marred by thin thought, vague description, and unnecessary length, were scarcely in print (1882), before they provoked his own critical renouncement, which was confirmed by an immediate change in practice. From 1879 to 1883 he focused his attention upon sonnets, writing three-fifths of his total of fifty-one. Between 1884 and 1891 he published only three poems like his early ones—represented here by "The Garden" (3)—and only five sonnets. During the same period, however, he published at least forty poems confined within four to twenty verses. This pattern, like Dickinson, he followed thereafter.

This change in external pattern was accompanied by important structural changes: fewer similes but more metaphors, fewer direct but more oblique statements, fewer images and phrases in series by way of rhetorical repetition and parallelism. His imagery became more and more functional; his structures, more and more compact. One aspect of this development, which is apparent in many poems (24, 31, 52, 55, 109, 142), long ago drew the comment of the English editor and critic, Harold J. Massingham. He championed Father Tabb as a successful Imagist poet before T. E. Hulme set the genre and Ezra Pound invented the term.

With these new elements came a different poetry—the kind Donne, Herbert, and Crashaw had introduced, the kind that Emily Dickinson was writing and keeping to herself, and the kind that has won the approval of our contemporaries. His finer poems are designed wholes and often the conceit is the structure; they are perfect units of acute sensibility (21, 38, 68, 99, 151, 168, 179, 183, 192, 208, 212). As to sense structure, they are essentially analytic and achieved through conceit, antithesis, paradox, oxymoron, hyperbole, and paranomasia; but as to sound structure, they are rather of the Romantic and Victorian periods than of the seventeenth century (21, 30, 37, 49, 51, 63, 76, 83, 102, 108, 125, 127, 141, 171, 181).

The union of the commonplace with the unusual, the trivial with the significant, the ugly with the beautiful, which enables the poet to combine several levels of thought and to direct attention forcefully to the one of his own choice by the very incongruity of the juxtaposition, is notably realized in many of Father Tabb's poems (21, 40, 51, 54, 59, 63, 66, 82, 124, 126, 140, 149, 180, 247). Examples, of course, abound in the work of Donne and Dickinson. How unprepared critics were in 1895 to recognize—what we now accept—the artistry of this manner, can easily be gauged from the reception accorded "Out of Bounds" (102). From the pen of Jeannette Gilder (*The Critic*, September 7, 1895) came this unqualified condemnation: "Father Tabb seems almost to have lost the faculty of distinguishing the true from the false, the sphere of faith from that of fancy. This state of mind . . . fairly burlesques itself in the preposterous conceit, flippantly entitled 'Out of Bounds.' For sheer buffoonery no medieval friar could have beaten that."

In all of these poems, it is evident, Father Tabb was continuously cultivating verbal economy; he was reducing his utterance to the barest skeleton of language. But he went further. The deviations from syntactical norms by his contemporaries Dickinson and Whitman are known and recognized. They are present in Tabb, but no one has as yet even pointed them out or seen their significance, not only in relation to the metaphysical aspect of composition, but also in themselves anticipating our present practice. He often did away with subject and principal verb, principal verb, subject and auxiliary verb, conjunction, relative pronoun, and put the burden of carrying the meaning on noun, adjective, phrase and subordinate clause. The chief reason for this paring to the syntactical bone was his consuming passion to express only the essence of his poetic contemplations and to embody them in the tightest of speech constructs.

One of the earliest examples of the omission of subject and principal verb is "Fancy" (43; also 48, 57, 109). A variation occurs in the use of a predicate adjective instead of a predicate noun, as in "The Nativity" which is structured as a contrast and a paradox (251; also 25, 64). Some poems omit all verbs; one of the best illustrations is likewise his most anthologized poem—"Evolution" (100). Another often-quoted quatrain notable for syntactical liberty is "The Dandelion" (72).

"St. Mary of Egypt" (5) is composed of four stanzas, of which the first, third, and fourth have normal sentence structures, but the second has only a series of elliptical verses (also 8, 12, 44, 79). This same elliptical structure aptly imparts to the opening lines of "Shell-Tints" (39) a colloquial tone, which is continued to the last stanza. The conversational touch is present in "Leaf and Soul" (210), which offers another pattern—the omission of subject and auxiliary verb. The subject is omitted in "Anonymous" (158); the principal verb in "The Assumption" (262). There is design in Father Tabb's employment of fragmentary sentences and prepositional and participial phrases. They may serve, at the beginning or at the end of his poems, as a summary of the idea or of the situation that induces his reflections or occasions the subsequent action. "Autumn Gold" (59) exemplifies the summary at the beginning, "Bethel" (184) at the beginning as well as at the end.

Because Father Tabb was an authentic poet and a self-reliant person, he moved away from some of the restricting forces of his own times to independent expression and interpretation. As his letters show, he was constantly critical of his own art and he was always reaching beyond his present achievement. The poems he wrote before Emily Dickinson's 1890 and 1894 volumes appeared, as well as after he knew her work, are sufficient warrant to include him among the American poets who experimented and to rank him as one of the earliest heralds of modern poetic form.

*   *   *

Of the nearly nine hundred serious poems written by Father Tabb, which can be found in the complete edition published in 1928, The Poetry of Father Tabb—now out of print—only those considered his best are reprinted here. None of his humorous verse in Child Verse and Quips and Quiddits is included. The arrangement in chronological order is based on dates given in manuscripts, mention in the poet's letters and in the letters of others, and inferences from substantiated premises.

1877–1882

1.

NEKROS

("During my father's last illness")

Lo! all thy glory gone!
God's masterpiece undone!
The last created and the first to fall;
The noblest, frailest, godliest of all.

Death seems the conqueror now,
And yet his victor thou;
The fatal shaft, its venom quenched in thee,
A mortal raised to immortality.

Child of the humble sod,
Wed with the breath of God,
Descend! for with the lowest thou must lie—
Arise! thou hast inherited the sky.

2.

SHELLEY

Shelley, the ceaseless music of thy soul
Breathes in the Cloud and in the Skylark's song,
That float as an embodied dream along
The dewy lids of morning. In the dole
That haunts the West Wind, in the joyous roll
Of Arethusan fountains, or among
The wastes where Ozymandias the strong
Lies in colossal ruin, thy control
Speaks in the wedded rhyme. Thy spirit gave
A fragrance to all nature and a tone
To inexpressive silence. Each apart—
Earth, Air, and Ocean—claims thee as its own;
The twain that bred thee, and the panting wave
That clasped thee like an overflowing heart.

[3]

3. THE GARDEN

I closed the gate at sunset, and alone,
As Adam once in Paradise, erewhile
The deep sleep fell upon him, talked with flowers.
All things had voices for me, and the dews
An even-song, in chorus, thus began:

We come and go as the breezes blow,
  But whence or where
Hath ne'er been told in the legends old
  By the dreaming seer.
We drip through the night, from the star-lids bright,
  On the sleeping flowers,
And deep in the breast is our perfumed rest
  Through the darkened hours;
But again with the day we are up and away,
  With our stolen dyes,
To paint all the shrouds of the drifting clouds
  In the western skies.

They ceased; and lo! the swinging violet bells
Rang requiem, in the purple tones of love.

  Our cradle was a maiden's grave,
  Where, just above her shrouded eyes,
  We looked upon the quiet skies,
  As whence the charm they gave.

  No lordly monument was there
  To mock the shrine of modest worth;
  We, kindred children of the earth,
  Alone its guardians were.

[4]

And all our genial presence tells
Remembrance of that heart beneath,
That, e'en in lethargy of death,
Oblivion repels.

A lily wept to hear them, and I turned
To find her pale with sorrow. She never spake,
Nor lifted up her glory: and I said:

Some subtle power is thine
    To teach this heart of mine,
In every charm to see
    The Hand that fashioned thee.

Long pulseless as in death,
    The veiling hours beneath,
Thy vital essence lay
    Unconscious of the day.

Till, with propitious skies,
    Thy Maker bade thee rise,
And to the wooing air
    Unfolded thy treasures rare.

Then swift the powers of light
    Their sevenfold gifts unite,
New glories to impart
    Beyond mimetic art,

Proclaiming to the eye
    A mystic harmony,
In silence that all sound
    Attunes to thought profound.

[5]

In God's eternal plan,
        Before the world began,
Thy mission was defined
        To raise the docile mind.

And if the spirit spurn
        Thy lesson meek to learn,
In judgment thou shalt rise
        To hurl it from the skies.

'Tis thus thou teachest me
        In reverence to see
With God is nothing small,
        Since all proclaim Him All.

Now twilight reigned. One star was in the west,
One lonely rose hung, sleeping on the stem,
And, with a parting murmur, thus I mused:

Thou hast not toiled, sweet Rose,
        Yet needest rest;
Softly thy petals close
        Upon thy breast,
Like folded hands, of labor long oppressed.

Naught knowest thou of sin,
        Yet tears are thine;
Baptismal drops within
        Thy chalice shine,
At morning's birth, at evening's calm decline.

Alas! one day hath told
        The tale to thee!

Thy tender leaves enfold
    Life's mystery:
Its shadow falls alike on thee and me!

4.   DAYBREAK

What was thy dream, sweet Morning? for, behold,
Thine eyes are heavy with the balm of night,
And, as reluctant lilies to the light,
The languid lids of lethargy unfold.
Was it the tale of yesterday retold—
An echo wakened from the western height,
Where the warm glow of sunset dalliance bright
Grew, with the pulse of waning passion, cold?
Or was it some heraldic vision grand
Of legends that forgotten ages keep
In twilight, where the sundering shoals of day
Vex the dim sails, unpiloted, of sleep,
Till, one by one, the freighting fancies gay,
Like bubbles, vanish on the treacherous strand?

5.   ST. MARY OF EGYPT

Strong to suffer, strong to sin,
    Loving much, and much forgiven,
In the desert realm a queen,
    Penance-crowned, to cope with Heaven,
Solitude alone could be
Room enough for God and thee.

Long the vigil, stern the fast;
    Morn, with night's anointing, chill;

Noon with passion overcast;
    Night with phantoms fouler still;
Prayer and penitential tears
Battling with the lust of years.

Low upon the parching sand,
    Shrivelled in the blight of day,
As beneath a throbbing brand
    Prone thy ghastly shadow lay,
Till the manacles of hell
From thy fevered spirit fell.

Then, O queen of solitude!
    Silence led thee as a bride,
Clothed anew in maidenhood,
    To an altar purified,
Lit with holy fires, to prove
Self the sacrifice of love.

6.   KEATS
          ("*The most adorable of poets*")
Upon thy tomb 'tis graven, "Here lies one
Whose name is writ in water." Could there be
A flight of fancy fitlier feigned for thee,
A fairer motto for her favorite son?
For, as the wave, thy varying numbers run—
Now crested proud in tidal majesty,
Now tranquil as the twilight reverie
Of some dim lake the white moon looks upon
While teems the world with silence. Even there,
In each Protean rainbow-tint that stains
The breathing canvas of the atmosphere,

We read an exhalation of thy strains.
Thus on the scroll of nature everywhere
Thy name, a deathless syllable, remains.

7.   THE FLOWERS

They are not ours,
The fleeting flowers,
But lights of God
That through the sod
Flash upwards from the world beneath—
That region peopled wide with death—
And tell us, in each subtle hue,
That life renewed is passing through
Our world again to seek the skies,
Its native realm of Paradise.

How brief their day!
They cannot stay;
Our mother earth
Beholds their birth
And spreads her ample bosom deep
Some relic of their stay to keep,
And each in benediction flings
A virtue from its dainty wings;
But lo! she treasures it in vain;
It blooms and vanishes again.

8.   UNMOORED

To die in sleep—to drift from dream to dream
Along the banks of slumber, beckoned on
Perchance by forms familiar, till anon,
Unconsciously, the ever-widening stream

Beyond the breakers bore thee, and the beam
Of everlasting morning woke upon
Thy dazzled gaze, revealing one by one
Thy visions grown immortal in its gleam.
O blessed consummation! thus to feel
In death no touch of terror. Tenderly
As shadows to the evening hills he came
In garb of God's dear messenger to thee,
Nor on thy weary eyelids broke the seal
In reverence for a brother's holier name.

9.   ASLEEP

        Nay, wake him not!
    Unfelt our presence near,
    Nor falls a whisper on his dreaming ear:
    He sees but sleep's celestial visions clear,
        All else forgot.

        And who shall say
    That in life's waking dream
    There be not ever near us those we deem
    (As now our faces to the sleeper seem)
        Far, far away?

10.   ENGADDI

Hail, trackless waste! a heart made desolate
Speeds from a sterner solitude to thee!
Oh, let me, lost in contemplation, be
Among thy children numbered—at the gate
Of Mercy, meekly pleading, still to wait,
With lifted eye and penitential knee,

The silent herald of Eternity—
The swift, relentless messenger of Fate!
Heaven weeps not here for man's ingratitude,
Where from the heart perpetual fountains flow;
But Love, in cloudless majesty revealed,
Sustains the soul with Hope's celestial food,
Till, life to Life, the flame supernal grow
And dust to dust the parting spirit yield.

11.   THE SHADOW
              (*"A favorite of Lanier's"*)
       O shadow, in thy fleeting form I see
       The friend of fortune that once clung to me.
       In flattering light thy constancy is shown;
       In darkness thou wilt leave me all alone.

12.   UNUTTERED
       Waiting for words—as on the broad expanse
       Of heaven the formless vapors of the night,
       Expectant, wait the oracle of light
       Interpreting their dumb significance;
       Or like a star that in the morning glance
       Shrinks, as a folding blossom, from the sight,
       Nor wakens till upon the western height
       The shadows to their evening towers advance—
       So, in my soul, a dream ineffable,
       Expectant of the sunshine or the shade,
       Hath oft, upon the brink of twilight chill,
       Or at the dawn's pale glimmering portal stayed
       In tears, that all the quivering eyelids fill,
       In smiles, that on the lip of silence fade.

13.   EASTER

Like a meteor, large and bright,
Fell a golden seed of light
On the field of Christmas night
        When the Babe was born;
Then 'twas sepulchred in gloom
Till above His holy tomb
Flashed its everlasting bloom—
        Flower of Easter morn.

14.   MISTLETOE

To the cradle-bough of a naked tree,
        Benumbed with ice and snow,
A Christmas dream brought suddenly
        A birth of mistletoe.

The shepherd stars from their fleecy cloud
        Strode out on the night to see;
The Herod north-wind blustered loud
        To rend it from the tree.

But the old year took it for a sign
        And blessed it in his heart:
"With prophecy of peace divine
        Let now my soul depart."

15.   GLIMPSES

As one who in the hush of twilight hears
The pausing pulse of nature, when the light
Commingles in the dim mysterious rite

Of darkness with the mutual pledge of tears,
Till soft, anon, one timorous star appears,
Pale-budding as the earliest blossom white
That comes in winter's livery bedight,
To hide the gifts of genial spring she bears—
So, unto me—what time the mysteries
Of consciousness and slumber weave a dream
And pause above it with abated breath,
Like intervals in music—lights arise,
Beyond prophetic nature's farthest gleam,
That teach me half the mystery of death.

16.   HOMELESS

Methinks that if my spirit could behold
Its earthly habitation void and chill,
Whence all its time-encircled good and ill
Expanded to eternity, 'twould fold
Its trembling pinions o'er the bosom cold,
Recalling there the pulses' wonted thrill,
And lean perchance to catch the echo still
That erst in life the dream of passion told.
How calm the dissolution! Could she spurn
Her spouse, so late, and brother? Could she trace
The strange, familiar lineaments, and mark
The doom of her own writing in the face,
To find, alas! no more the vital spark,
Nor breathe one sigh of pity to return?

17.   SHAKESPEARE'S MOURNERS

I saw the grave of Shakespeare in a dream,
And round about it grouped a wondrous throng,
His own majestic mourners, who belong
Forever to the Stage of Life, and seem
The rivals of reality. Supreme
Stood Hamlet, as erewhile the graves among,
Mantled in thought; and sad Ophelia sung
The same swan-dirge she chanted in the stream.
Othello, dark in destiny's eclipse,
Laid on the tomb a lily. Near him wept
Dejected Constance. Fair Cordelia's lips
Moved prayerfully the while her father slept,
And each and all, inspired of vital breath,
Kept vigil o'er the sacred spoils of death.

1883

18.   THE PETREL

("*During forty days at sea between Baltimore
and Rio this bird was always seen.*")

A wanderer o'er the sea-graves ever green,
Whereon the foam-flowers blossom day by day,
Thou flittest as a doomful shadow gray
That from the wave no sundering light can wean.
What wouldst thou from the deep unfathomed glean,
Frail voyager, and whither leads the way?
Or art thou, as the sailor legends say,
An exile from the spirit-world unseen?
Lo! desolate, above a colder tide,
Pale memory, a sea-bird like to thee,
Flits outward where the whitening billows hide
What seemed of life the one reality—
A mist whereon the morning bloom hath died,
Returning, ghost-like, to the restless sea.

19.   THE HALF-RING MOON

Over the sea, over the sea,
My love he is gone to a far countrie;
But he brake a golden ring with me
        The pledge of his faith to be.

Over the sea, over the sea,
He comes no more from the far countrie;
But at night, where the new moon loved to be,
        Hangs the half of a ring for me.

1884

20.   EASTER LILIES

    Though long in wintry sleep ye lay,
    The powers of darkness could not stay
    Your coming at the call of day,
        Proclaiming spring.

    Nay, like the faithful virgins wise,
    With lamps replenished ye arise,
    Ere dawn the death-anointed eyes
        Of Christ the King.

21.   THE RING

    Hold the trinket near thine eye,
    And it circles earth and sky;
    Place it further, and behold!
    But a finger's breadth of gold.

    Thus our lives, beloved, lie
    Ringed with love's fair boundary;
    Place it further, and its sphere
    Measures but a falling tear.

22.   ROBIN

Come to me, Robin! The daylight is dying!
      Come to me now!
Come, ere the cypress-tree over me sighing,
Dank with the shadow-tide, circle my brow;
Come, ere oblivion speed to me, flying
      Swifter than thou!

Come to me, Robin! The far echoes waken
    Cold to my cry!
Oh! with the swallow-wing, love overtaken,
Hence to the echo-land, homeward to fly!
Thou art my life, Robin. Oh! love-forsaken,
    How can I die?

23.   BROTHERHOOD

Knew not the Sun, sweet Violet,
    The while he gleaned the snow,
That thou in darkness sepulchred
    Wast slumbering below?
Or spun a splendor of surprise
Around him to behold thee rise?

Saw not the Star, sweet Violet,
    What time a drop of dew
Let fall his image from the sky
    Into the deeper blue?
Nor waxed he tremulous and dim
When rival Dawn supplanted him?

And dreamest thou, sweet Violet,
    That I, the vanished Star,
The Dewdrop, and the morning Sun
    Thy closest kinsmen are—
So near that, waking or asleep,
We each and all thy image keep?

24.   THE WATER-LILY

Whence, O fragrant form of light,
Hast thou drifted through the night,
Swanlike, to a leafy nest,
On the restless waves, at rest?

Art thou from the snowy zone
Of a mountain-summit blown,
Or the blossom of a dream,
Fashioned in the foamy stream?

Nay, methinks the maiden moon,
When the daylight came too soon,
Fleeting from her bath to hide,
Left her garment in the tide.

25.   MILTON

So fair thy vision that the night
Abided with thee, lest the light,
A flaming sword before thine eyes,
Had shut thee out of Paradise.

1885

26. ## TO A PHOTOGRAPH

O tender shade!
Lone captive of enamoured light,
That from an angel visage bright
    A glance betrayed.

    Dost thou not sigh
To wander from thy prison-place?
To seek again the vanished face,
    Or else, to die?

    A shadow like thee,
Dim Eidolon—a dream disproved—
A memory of light removed,
    Behold in me!

27. ## PHANTOMS

Are ye the ghosts of fallen leaves,
    O flakes of snow,
For which through naked trees the winds
    A-mourning go?

Or are ye angels, bearing home
    The host unseen
Of truant spirits, to be clad
    Again in green?

28. ## KILLDEE

("*Heard at home in Virginia*")

Killdee! Killdee! far o'er the lea
    At twilight comes the cry.

Killdee! a marsh-mate answereth
        Across the shallow sky.

Killdee! Killdee! thrills over me
        A rhapsody of light,
As star to star gives utterance
        Between the day and night.

Killdee! Killdee! O memory,
        The twin birds, joy and pain,
Like shadows parted by the sun,
        At twilight meet again!

29.   MARY

Maid-Mother of humanity divine,
Alone thou art in thy supremacy,
Since God Himself did reverence to thee
And built of flesh a temple one with thine,
Wherein, through all eternity, to shrine
His inexpressive glory. Blessed be
The miracle of thy maternity,
Of grace the sole immaculate design!
Lo! earth and heaven—the footstool and the throne
Of Him who bowed obedient to thy sway,
What time in lowly Nazareth, unknown,
He led of life the long-sequestered way—
Pause, till their tongues are tutored of thine own,
"Magnificat" in wondering love to say.

30.   ST. AFRA TO THE FLAMES

Here, on the prey of passion, famished Flames,
Feed here! Spare not your victim. Torture tames

The wanton flesh rebellious. Let the heat
Of these your fierce caresses free the feet
And loose the fettered pinions of desire.
Delay not! leap the barriers and fire
The citadel, the heart. A flame is there
To which your kiss is coldness. Clothe me fair,
O Christ, with purple penance. Crown me queen
Of agonies that cleave all mists between
My God and me! Life's vintage drop by drop
Fast fills the destined measure of my cup.
Quaff, Lord, my potion! Pledge me, and thy breath
Shall sweeten all the bitterness of death.

31. ## THE REAPER

Tell me whither, maiden June,
Down the dusky slope of noon
With thy sickle of a moon,
    Goest thou to reap.

"Fields of Fancy by the stream
Of night in silvery silence gleam,
To heap with many a harvest-dream
    The granary of Sleep."

32. ## THE LONELY MOUNTAIN
(*"Each year I find it so—some missing voice for me."*)

One bird, that ever with the wakening spring
    Was wont to sing,
I wait, through all my woodlands, far and near,
    In vain to hear.

The voice of many waters, silent long,
        Breaks forth in song:
Young breezes to the listening leaves outpour
        Their heavenly lore;

A thousand other winged warblers sweet,
        Returning, greet
Their fellows, and rebuild upon my breast
        The wonted nest.

But unto me one fond familiar strain
        Comes not again—
A breath whose faintest echo, farthest heard,
        A mountain stirred.

1887

33.   INDIAN SUMMER
("*Often observed from my window, looking to the left.*")
'Tis said, in death, upon the face
Of age, a momentary trace
Of infancy's returning grace
    Forestalls decay;

And here, in Autumn's dusky reign,
A birth of blossom seems again
To flush the woodland's fading train
    With dreams of May.

34.   NARCISSUS
The god enamoured never knew
The shadow that beguiled his view,
Nor deemed it less divinely true
    Than Life and Love.

And so the poet, while he wrought
His image in the tide of thought,
Deemed it a glimpse in darkness caught
    Of light above.

35.   A CHRISTMAS CRADLE
Let my heart the cradle be
Of Thy bleak Nativity!
Tossed by wintry tempests wild,
If it rock Thee, Holy Child,
Then, as grows the outer din,
Greater peace shall reign within.

1888

36.   A LENTEN THOUGHT
Alone with Thee, who canst not be alone,
    At midnight, in Thine everlasting day;
Lo, less than naught, of nothingness undone,
    I, prayerless, pray!

Behold—and with Thy bitterness make sweet,
    What sweetest is in bitterness to hide—
Like Magdalen, I grovel at Thy feet
    In lowly pride.

Smite, till my wounds beneath Thy scourging cease;
    Soothe, till my heart in agony hath bled;
Nor rest my soul with enmity at peace,
    Till death be dead.

37.   THE CHORD
        In this narrow cloister bound
        Dwells a sisterhood of sound,
        Far from alien voices rude
        As in secret solitude.
        Unisons, that yearned apart,
        Here, in harmony of heart,
        Blend divided sympathies,
        And in choral strength arise,
        Like the cloven tongues of fire,
        One in heavenly desire.

38.   MAGDALEN
            (*After Swinburne*)
        "She hath done what she could."
It was thus that He spake of her,

Trembling and pale as the penitent stood.
"And this she hath done shall be told for the sake of her,
Told as embalmed in the gift that I take of her,
   Take, as an earnest of all that she would
   Who hath done what she could."

"She hath done what she could";
Lo, the flame that hath driven her
   Downward, is quenched! and her grief like a flood
In the strength of a rain-swollen torrent hath shriven her.
Much hath she loved and much is forgiven her;
   Love in the longing fulfills what it would—
   "She hath done what she could."

39.   SHELL-TINTS

            Sea-shell, whence the rainbow dyes,
            Flashing in thy sunset skies?
            Thou wast in the penal brine
            When appeared the saving sign.
            "Yea, but when the bow was bended,
            Hope, that hung it in the sky,
            Down into the deep descended
            Where the starless shadows lie;
            And with tender touch of glory
            Traced in living lines of love,
            On my lowly walls, the story
            Written in the heavens above."

40.   FATHER DAMIEN

            O God, the cleanest offering
               Of tainted earth below,
            Unblushing to Thy feet we bring—
               "A leper white as snow!"

1889

41.   AN INFLUENCE
I see thee—heaven's unclouded face
    A vacancy around thee made,
Its sunshine a subservient grace
    Thy lovelier light to shade.

I feel thee, as the billows feel
    A river freshening the brine;
A life's libation poured to heal
    The bitterness of mine.

42.   SELECTION
Among the trees, O God,
    Is there not one
That with unrivalled love
    Thou look'st upon?

And of all blessed birds,
    Hath not thy love
Found for its fittest mate
    The homing dove?

Or, 'mid the flame of flowers
    That light the land,
Doth not the lily first
    Before thee stand?

So says my soul, O God,
    The type of thee:
"In each life-circle, one
    Was made for me."

43.   FANCY

A boat unmoored, wherein a dreamer lies,
    The slumberous waves low-lisping of a land
Where love, forever with unclouded eyes,
    Goes, wed with wandering music, hand in hand.

44.   JOY
        (*"Written one Saturday afternoon while keeping
                five o'clock study."*)
            New-born, how long to stay?
            The while a dewdrop may
                Or rainbow-gleam:
            One kiss of sun or shade,
            And lo, the breath that made
                Unmakes the dream!

45.   TO THE BABE NIVA
        (*"Written on hearing of the death of Niva, the infant
        daughter of Mr. Wynans, buried in the deep snow."*)
            Niva, Child of Innocence,
                Dust to dust we go;
            Thou, when winter wooed thee hence,
                Wentest snow to snow.

1890

46.   WESTWARD

("On Willie's [William McDevitt's] going
to the West to live.")

And dost thou lead him hence with thee,
    O setting sun,
And leave the shadows all to me
    When he is gone?
Ah, if my grief his guerdon be,
    My dark his light,
I count each loss felicity
    And bless the night.

47.   CHILD AND MOTHER

Look on Thy Mother's face,
That miracle of grace,
    O Son Divine!
That, bending, she may see
A greater mystery
    Revealed in Thine.

Without Thee, she had been
Nor Mother Blessed nor Queen;
    Nor wouldest Thou,
Her lowliness apart,
Have borne the Human Heart
    Thou bearest now.

Then, if I render love
Through her, Thou must approve
    The tribute paid;
For 'tis Thy Holy Face,
Not Caesar's, that I trace
    In hers portrayed.

[45]

48.   DECEMBER

Dull sky above, dead leaves below,
And hungry winds that whining go,
Like faithful hounds upon the track
Of one beloved that comes not back.

1891

49.   THE RECOMPENSE

She brake the box, and all the house was filled
      With waftures from the fragrant store thereof,
While at His feet a costlier vase distilled
      The bruised balm of penitential love.

And, lo, as if in recompense of her,
      Bewildered in the lingering shades of night,
He breaks anon the sealed sepulchre,
      And fills the world with rapture and with light.

50.   INTIMATIONS

I knew the flowers had dreamed of you
      And hailed the morning with regret,
For all their faces with the dew
      Of vanished joy were wet.

I knew the winds had passed your way,
      Though not a sound the truth betrayed;
About their pinions all the day
      A summer fragrance stayed.

And so, awaking or asleep,
      A memory of lost delight
By day the sightless breezes keep
      And silent flowers by night.

[49]

51.   **THE BUBBLE**

("*Suggested on the anniversary of Father Menu's death.*")

Why should I stay? Nor seed nor fruit have I.
But, sprung at once to beauty's perfect round,
Nor loss, nor gain, nor change in me is found—
A life-complete in death-complete to die.

52.   **THE HUMMING-BIRD**

A flash of harmless lightning,
    A mist of rainbow dyes,
The burnished sunbeams brightening,
    From flower to flower he flies;

While wakes the nodding blossom,
    But just too late to see
What lip hath touched her bosom
    And drained her nectary.

53.   **INSOMNIA**

E'en this, Lord, didst Thou bless—
This pain of sleeplessness—
    The livelong night,
Urging God's gentlest angel from thy side,
That anguish only might with thee abide
    Until the light.

Yea, e'en the last and best,
Thy victory and rest,
   Came thus to thee;
For 'twas while others calmly slept around,
That thou alone in sleeplessness was found,
    To comfort me.

54.   A BUNCH OF ROSES

The rosy mouth and rosy toe
    Of little baby brother
Until about a month ago
    Had never met each other;
But nowadays the neighbors sweet,
    In every sort of weather,
Half way with rosy fingers meet
    To kiss and play together.

55.   THE BUTTERFLY

Leafless, stemless, floating flower,
From a rainbow's scattered bower,
Like a bubble of the air
Blown by fairies, tell me where
Seed or scion I may find
Bearing blossoms of thy kind.

1892

56.   THE SNOWDROP
                (Father Damien)
      "A Nun of Winter's sisterhood,"
      A snowdrop in the garden stood
      Alone amid the solitude
              That round her lay.

      No sister blossom there was seen;
      No memory of what had been;
      No promise of returning green,
              Or scented spray:

      But she alone was bold to bear
      The banner of the spring, and dare,
      In winter's stern despite, declare
              A gentler sway.

      So didst thou, Damien, when the glow
      Of faith and hope was waning low,
      For souls bewintered dare the snow
              And lead the way.

57.   POETRY

      A gleam of heaven; the passion of a star
              Held captive in the clasp of harmony;
      A silence, shell-like breathing from afar
              The rapture of the deep—eternity.

58.   LOVE'S AUTOGRAPH

          Once only did he pass my way.
              "When wilt thou come again?

Ah, leave some token of thy stay!"
He wrote (and vanished) "Pain."

59.   AUTUMN-GOLD

Death in the house, and the golden-rod
    A-bloom in the field!
O blossom, how, from the lifeless clod,
When the fires are out and the ashes cold,
Doth a vein that the miners know not yield
    Such wealth of gold?

60.   MATURITY

Talk not of childhood's thoughtless joy!
I would not be again a boy
        For all that boyhood brings;
The callow fledgling in the nest
Is not of birds supremely blest
        As he that soars and sings.

61.   COMMUNION

Once when my heart was passion-free
        To learn of things divine,
The soul of nature suddenly
        Outpoured itself in mine.

I held the secrets of the deep
        And of the heavens above;
I knew the harmonies of sleep,
        The mysteries of love.

And for a moment's interval
    The earth, the sky, the sea—
My soul encompassed, each and all,
    As now they compass me.

To one in all, to all in one—
    Since love the work began—
Life's ever-widening circles run,
    Revealing God and man.

62.   TO THE SPHINX

Ah, not alone in Egypt's desert land
    Thy dwelling-place apart!
But wheresoe'er the scorching passion-sand
    Hath seared the human heart.

63.   "IS THY SERVANT A DOG?"

So must he be who in the crowded street,
Where shameless Sin and flaunting Pleasure meet,
Amid the noisome footprints finds the sweet
    Faint vestige of Thy feet.

64.   BETTER

Better for sin to dwell from heaven apart
    In foulest night
Than on its lidless eyeballs feel the dart
    Of torturing light.
Better to pine in floods of sulphurous fire
    Than far above

Behold the bliss of satisfied desire,
    Nor taste thereof.
Yea, love is lord, e'en where the powers of pain
    Undying dwell;
Defiled, in spotless glory to remain
    Were deeper hell.

65.   LOVE'S HYBLA

My thoughts fly to thee, as the bees
    To find their favorite flower;
Then home, with honeyed memories
    Of many a fragrant hour;

For with thee is the place apart
    Where sunshine ever dwells,
The Hybla, whence my hoarding heart
    Would fill its wintry cells.

66.   COMPENSATION

How many an acorn falls to die
    For one that makes a tree!
How many a heart must pass me by
    For one that clings to me!

How many a suppliant wave of sound
    Must still unheeded roll
For one low utterance that found
    An echo in my soul!

67. ## AT LANIER'S GRAVE

I stand beside a comrade tree
That guards the spot where thou art laid;
For since thy light is lost to me
    I loiter in the shade.
I lean upon the rugged stone
As on the breast from whence I came,
To learn 'tis not my heart alone
    That bears thy sacred name.

68. ## CONFIDED

Another lamb, O Lamb of God, behold,
Within this quiet fold,
Among Thy Father's sheep
I lay to sleep!
A heart that never for a night did rest
Beyond its mother's breast.
Lord, keep it close to Thee,
Lest waking it should bleat and pine for me!

69. ## A CRADLE-SONG

Sing it, Mother! sing it low;
    Deem it not an idle lay.
In the heart 'twill ebb and flow
    All the life-long way.

Sing it, Mother! softly sing,
    While he slumbers on thy knee;
All that after-years may bring
    Shall flow back to thee.

Sing it, Mother, love is strong!
When the tears of manhood fall,
Echoes of thy cradle-song
Shall its peace recall.

Sing it, Mother! when his ear
Catcheth first the Voice Divine,
Dying, he may smile to hear
What he deemeth thine.

70.   CHRIST THE MENDICANT

A stranger, to His own
He came; and one alone,
Who knew not sin,
His lowliness believed,
And in her soul conceived
To let Him in.

He naked was, and she
Of her humanity
A garment wove.
He hungered; and she gave,
What most His heart did crave—
A Mother's love.

71.   THE LAKE
("*Our quondam lake—written one Saturday afternoon
while keeping five o'clock study.*")
I am a lonely woodland lake;
The trees that round me grow,
The glimpse of heaven above me, make
The sum of all I know.

The mirror of their dreams to be
    Alike in shade and shine,
To clasp in love's captivity,
    And keep them one—is mine.

72.   DANDELION

With locks of gold today;
Tomorrow, silver gray;
Then blossom-bald. Behold,
O man, thy fortune told!

73.   PREJUDICE

A leaf may hide the largest star
    From love's uplifted eye;
A mote of prejudice out-bar
    A world of charity.

74.   EARTH'S TRIBUTE

First the grain and then the blade—
The one destroyed, the other made;
Then stalk and blossom, and again
The gold of newly minted grain.

So life, by death the reaper cast
To earth, again shall arise at last;
For 'tis the service of the sod
To render God the things of God.

[61]

75. THE WHITE JASMINE

*("Written near Ellicott City under an umbrella. The young
girl lived in a house off the Frederick Pike near
the college. She was dying.")*

I knew she lay above me,
    Where the casement all the night
Shone, softened with a phosphor glow
    Of sympathetic light,
And that her fledgling spirit pure
    Was pluming fast for flight.

Each tendril throbbed and quickened
    As I nightly climbed apace,
And could scarce restrain the blossoms
    When, anear the destined place,
Her gentle whisper thrilled me
    Ere I gazed upon her face.

I waited, darkling, till the dawn
    Should touch me into bloom,
While all my being panted
    To outpour its first perfume,
When, lo! a paler flower than mine
    Had blossomed in the gloom.

76. THE INCARNATION

Save through the flesh Thou wouldst not come to me—
The flesh, wherein Thy strength my weakness found
A weight to bow Thy Godhead to the ground,
And lift to heaven a lost humanity.

77.   THE LARK

He rose and singing passed from sight:
    A shadow kindling with the sun,
His joy ecstatic flamed, till light
    And heavenly song were one.

78.   HOLY GROUND

Pause where apart the fallen sparrow lies,
    And lightly tread;
For there the pity of a Father's eyes
    Enshrines the dead.

79.   BLOSSOM

For this the fruit, for this the seed,
    For this the parent tree;
The least to man, the most to God—
    A fragrant mystery
Where love, with beauty glorified,
    Forgets utility.

80.   THE PRECURSOR

"As John of old before His face did go
To make the rough ways smooth, that all might know
The level road that leads to Bethlehem, lo,
I come," proclaims the snow.

81.   ANGELS OF PAIN

*("Reflections on a long illness in Baltimore from
September 1869 to January 1870.")*

Ah, should they come revisiting the spot
    Whence by our prayers we drove them utterly,
Shame were it for their saddened eyes to see
    How soon their visitations are forgot.

82.   THE SEA BUBBLE

    Yea, a bubble though I be,
    Love, O man, that fashioned thee
    Of the dust created me
    Not of earth, but of the sea:
    Kindred blossoms then are we—
    Time-blooms on eternity.

83.   SILENCE

Temple of God, from all eternity
Alone like Him without beginning found;
Of time and space and solitude the bound,
Yet in thyself of all communion free.
Is, then, the temple holier than He
That dwells therein? Must reverence surround
With barriers the portals lest a sound
Profane it? Nay; behold a mystery!
What was, abides; what is, hath ever been;
The lowliest the loftiest sustains.
A silence, by no breath of utterance stirred—
Virginity in motherhood—remains,
Clear, midst a cloud of all-pervading sin,
The voice of love's unutterable word.

[64]

THE DEBTOR CHRIST

What, woman, is my debt to thee
That I should not deny
The boon thou dost demand of me?
"I gave Thee power to die."

1893

85.   FORMATION

Whate'er we love becomes of us a part;
    The center of all tributary powers—
Our life is fed from nature's throbbing heart,
    And of her best the fibred growth is ours.

86.   WHISPER

Close cleaving unto silence, into sound
    She ventures as a timorous child from land,
Still glancing, at each step, around,
    Lest suddenly she lose her sister's hand.

87.   SUBMISSION

    Since to my smiting enemy
        Thou biddest me be meek,
Lo, gladlier, my God, to Thee
        I turn the other cheek.

88.   THE PORTRAIT

Each has his Angel-Guardian. Mine, I know,
Looks on me from that pictured face. Behold,
How clear, between those rifted clouds of gold,
The radiant brow! It is the morning glow
Of innocence ere yet the heart let go
The leading-strings of heaven. Upon the eyes
No shadow; like the restful noonday skies
They sanctify the teeming world below.
Why bows my soul before it? None but thou,
O tender child, has known the life estranged

From thee and all that made thy days of joy
The measure of my own. Behold me now—
That man that begs a blessing of the boy—
His very *self*; but from himself how changed!

89.   TO THE CHRIST

("*Especially commended by Mr. Chadwick
and old Dr. Furness.*")
Thou hast on earth a Trinity—
Thyself, my fellow-man, and me;
When one with him, then one with Thee;
Nor save together Thine are we.

90.   TO MY SHADOW

Friend forever in the light
    Cleaving to my side,
Harbinger of endless night,
    That must soon betide;

"Hither," seemest thou to say,
    "From the twilight now;
In the darkness when I stay,
    Never thence wilt thou."

91.   THE AGONY

I wrestled, as did Jacob, till the dawn,
With the reluctant Spirit of the Night
That keeps the keys of Slumber. Worn and white,
We paused a panting moment, while anon
The darkness paled around us. Thereupon—

His mighty limbs relaxing in affright—
The Angel pleaded: "Lo, the morning light!
O Israel, release me and begone!"
Then said I, "Nay, a captive to my will
I hold thee till the blessing thou dost keep
Be mine." Whereat he breathed upon my brow;
And, as the dew upon the twilight hill,
So on my spirit, over-wearied now,
Came tenderly the benediction, sleep.

92.   "VOX CLAMANTIS"

O sea, forever calling to the shore
        With menace or caress—
A voice like his unheeded that of yore
        Cried in the wilderness;
A deep forever yearning unto deep,
        For silence out of sound—
Thy restlessness the cradle of a sleep
        That thou hast never found.

93.   THE PROMONTORY

Not all the range of sea-born liberty
        Hath ever for one restless wave sufficed;
So pants the heart—of all compulsion free—
        Self-driven to the Rock, its barrier, Christ.

94.   THE CAPTIVES
("*Suggested by a Point Lookout experience, where I first
    heard Lanier's flute, before I met the player.*")
        Apart forever dwelt the twain,
        Save for one oft-repeated strain

Wherein what love alone could say
They learned and lavished day by day.

Strangers in all but misery
And music's hope-sustaining tie,
They lived and loved and died apart,
But soul to soul and heart to heart.

95.   KEATS-SAPPHO

Methinks, when first the nightingale
Was mated to thy deathless song,
That Sappho with emotion pale,
    Amid the Olympian throng,
Again, as in the Lesbian grove,
Stood listening with lips apart
To hear in thy melodious love
    The pantings of her heart.

96.   THE STATUE

First fashioned in the artist's brain,
It stood as in the marble vein,
    Revealed to him alone;
Nor could he from its native night
Have led it to the living light,
    Save through the lifeless stone.

E'en so, of silence and sound
A twin-born mystery is found,
    Like as of death and birth;

Without the pause we had not heard
The harmony, nor caught the word
That heaven reveals to earth.

97.   GOLDEN-ROD

As Israel in days of old
    Beneath the prophet's rod
Amid the waters, backward rolled,
    A path triumphant trod;
So, while thy lifted staff appears,
    Her pilgrim steps to guide,
The Autumn journeys on, nor fears
    The Winter's threatening tide.

98.   LIMITATIONS
("The best of my work, according to my judgment")
            Breathe above me or below,
            Never canst thou farther go
            Than the spirit's octave-span,
            Harmonizing God and Man.

            Thus within the iris-bound,
            Light a prisoner is found;
            Thus within my soul I see
            Life in time's captivity.

99.   THE POSTULANT

In ashes from the wasted fires of noon,
    Aweary of the light,
Comes Evening, a tearful novice, soon
    To take the veil of night.

[73]

100.   EVOLUTION

              Out of the dusk a shadow,
                  Then a spark;
              Out of the cloud a silence,
                  Then a lark;
              Out of the heart a rapture,
                  Then a pain;
              Out of the dead, cold ashes,
                  Life again.

101.   TO AN OLD WASSAIL-CUP

              Where Youth and Laughter lingered long
              To quaff delight, with wanton song
                  And warm caress,
              Now Time and Silence strive amain
              With lips unsatisfied to drain
                  Life's emptiness!

102.   OUT OF BOUNDS

          ("*Written one Christmas in the Chapel at St. Charles
          and suggested by the Infant over the altar.*")

              A little Boy of heavenly birth,
                  But far from home today,
              Comes down to find His ball, the Earth,
                  That Sin has cast away.
              O comrades, let us one and all
              Join in to get Him back His ball!

103. CHRIST TO THE VICTIM-TREE

Soon but not alone to die,
    Kinsman tree,
Limbed and lifeless must thou lie,
    Doomed, alas, for Me;
Yea, for Me, as I for all,
Must thou first a victim fall.

Thou for Me the bitter fruit
    Loth to bear,
Must of Death's accursed root
    Shame reluctant share.
Thus the Father's will divine
Seals thy fate to compass Mine.

1894

104.   FERN SONG

("*It was in my window, and grows still in the woods near
                    our lake.*")

          Dance to the beat of the rain, little Fern,
                And spread out your palms again,
                And say, "Though the sun
                Hath my vesture spun,
          He had labored, alas, in vain
                But for the shade
                That the Cloud hath made
          And the gift of the Dew and the Rain."
                Then laugh and upturn
                All your frounds, little Fern,
          And rejoice with the beat of the rain!

105.   STAR-JESSAMINE

          Discerning star from sister star,
                We give to each its name;
          But ye, O countless blossoms, are
                In fragrance and in flame
          So like that He from whom ye came
          Alone discerneth each by name.

106.   FAME

          Their noonday never knows
                What names immortal are;
          'Tis night alone that shows
                How star surpasseth star.

107. **WILD FLOWERS**

We grow where none but God,
    Life's Gardener,
Upon the sterile sod
    Bestows His care.

Our morn and evening dew—
    The sacrament
That maketh all things new—
    From heaven is sent;

And thither, ne'er in vain,
    We look for aid,
To find the punctual rain
    Or sun or shade,

Appointed hour by hour,
    To every need,
Alike of parent flower
    Or nursling seed;

Till, blossom-duty done,
    With parting smile,
We vanish, one by one,
    To sleep awhile.

108. **MY MESSMATE**

Why fear thee, brother Death,
That sharest, breath by breath,
This brimming life of mine?
Each draught that I resign
Into thy chalice flows.

Comrades of old are we;
All that the Present knows
Is but a shade of me:
My *Self* to thee alone
And to the Past is known.

109.   THE IMMACULATE CONCEPTION

A dewdrop of the darkness born,
      Wherein no shadow lies;
The blossom of a barren thorn,
      Whereof no petal dies;
A rainbow beauty passion-free,
Wherewith was veiled Divinity.

110.   THE BROOK

It is the mountain to the sea
That makes a messenger of me;
And, lest I loiter on the way
And lose what I am sent to say,
He sets his reverie to song
And bids me sing it all day long.
Farewell! for here the stream is slow,
And I have many a mile to go.

111.   BEETHOVEN AND ANGELO

One made the surging sea of tone
      Subservient to his rod;
One from the sterile womb of stone
      Raised children unto God.

[81]

112. REGRET

What pleading passion of the dark
    Hath left the Morning pale?
She listens! " 'Tis, alas, the Lark,
    And not the Nightingale!
O for the gloom-encircled sphere,
    Whose solitary bird
Outpours for Love's awakening ear
    What noon hath never heard!"

113. WAYFARERS

O comrade Sun, that day by day
Dost weave a shadow on my way,
Lest in the luxury of light
My soul forget the neighboring night,
Wilt thou whene'er, my journey done,
Thou wanderest our path upon,
Bear in thy beams a memory
Of one who walked the world with thee,
Or mourn amid the lavishness
Of life one hovering shade the less?

114. "OMNIPOTENCE IN BOUNDS"

Thou that couldst ne'er be bound
    Canst never more be free:
So close about Thee wound
    Is our humanity.
As well desert Thy Father's throne
As Mary's Motherhood disown.

115.   THE MID-DAY MOON
          Behold, whatever wind prevail,
          Slow westering, a phantom sail—
          The lonely soul of yesterday—
          Unpiloted, pursues her way.

116.   GOD'S LIKENESS
      Not in mine own but in my neighbor's face
              Must I Thine image trace;
      Nor he in his but in the light of mine
              Behold Thy Face Divine.

117.   MY MEDIATOR
          "None betwixt God and me?"
          "Behold, my neighbor, thee,
          Unto His lofty throne
          He makes my stepping-stone."

118.   THE MID-SEA SUN
      No peak to hide his splendor, till the day
              Has passed away;
      No dial shade of any tree or flower
              To mark the hour:
      A wave his orient cradle, and a wave
              His western grave.

119.   THE PRECIPICE
          Above the unfathomed deep
          Of Death we move in sleep,
          And who among us knows
          How near the brink he goes?

[83]

120.   THE ANGEL'S CHRISTMAS QUEST

"Where have ye laid my Lord?
Behold I find Him not!
Hath He, in heaven adored,
    His home forgot?
Give me, O sons of men,
My truant God again!"

"A voice from sphere to sphere—
A faltering murmur—ran,
'Behold, He is not here!
    Perchance with Man,
The lowlier made than we,
He hides His Majesty.' "

Then, hushed in wondering awe,
The spirit held his breath
And bowed; for, lo, he saw
    O'ershadowing Death,
A Mother's hand above,
Swathing the limbs of Love!

121.   IMMORTELLES

"They toil not, neither do they spin"—
The blossom-thoughts that here within
The garden of my soul arise;
Alike unheeding wintry skies,
Or sun or rain, or night or day,
And never hence to pass away.

122. MIDNIGHT

A flood of darkness overwhelms the land;
And all that God had planned,
Of loveliness beneath the noonday skies,
A dream o'ershadowed lies.

Amid the universal darkness deep
Only the Isles of Sleep,
As did the dwellings of the Israelite
In Egypt, stem the night.

123. CLOVER

Little masters, hat in hand,
Let me in your presence stand
Till your silence solve for me
This your threefold mystery.

Tell me—for I long to know—
How, in darkness there below,
Was your fairy fabric spun,
Spread, and fashioned, three in one.

Did your gossips gold and blue,
Sky and Sunshine, choose for you,
Ere your triple forms were seen,
Suited liveries of green?

Can ye—if ye dwelt indeed
Captives of a prison seed—
Like the Genie, once again
Get you back into the grain?

Little masters, may I stand
In your presence, hat in hand,
Waiting till you solve for me
This your threefold mystery?

124.   TO A BROTHER-BONE

Apart, of death and silence, we,
    The fittest emblems found,
Together, mad with minstrelsy,
    Leap into life and sound.

125.   MY OFFERING

He asked me bread, the bread whereby alone
    The beggar Love could live;
        I gave a stone.
He asked me fish, and I, a Passion's slave
    (All that I had to give),
        A serpent gave.
Then came His benediction: "Lo, in Me,
    A Stone retributive,
        A Serpent, see!"

1895

126.   MIGNONETTE

Give me the earth, and I might heap
    A mountain from the plain;
Give me the waters of the deep,
    I might their strength restrain:
But here a secret of the sod
Betrays the daintier hand of God.

127.   PAIN

I am a gardener to weed
    And dig about the heart;
To plant therein the pregnant seed,
    And watch, with many a smart,
The stem and leaf and blossom rise,
    Alternate to supply
The victims for the sacrifice,
    And, for the fruit, to die.

128.   OUTSPEEDED

Tonight the onward-rushing train
    Would bear thee far from me;
But, winged with swifter dreams, again
    My spirit flies to thee.

Nay, speeding far beyond thee, waits
    To welcome thee anew,
Where dawn is opening the gates
    To let the darkness through.

129.   THE ARCTIC

Is it a shroud or bridal veil
    That hides it from our sight,
The lonely sepulchre of day
    Or banquet-hall of night?

Are those the lights of revelry
    That glimmer o'er the deep
Or flashes of a funeral pyre
    Above the corpse of sleep?

Beyond those peaks impregnable
    Of everlasting snow
One star, a steadfast beacon, burns
    To guard the coast below.

Whence come the ghostly galleons
    The pirate sun to brave
And furl the shadowy flag of death
    Above a warmer grave?

130.   THE RAINBOW

What fruit of all thy blossom shed
    Remaineth unto me?
"A dream, whereon thy fancy fed,
Shall spin anon her golden thread,
    And then, of fetters free,
Arise with radiant pinions spread
    To heights of poesy."

[90]

131.

CHERRY BLOOM

Frailest and first to stand
Upon the border-land
    From darkness shriven,
In livery of death
Thou utterest the breath
    And light of heaven.

Though profitless thou seem
As doth a poet's dream,
    Apart from thee
Nor limb nor laboring root
May load with ripened fruit
    The parent tree.

132.

SELF-SACRIFICE

Lo, all I have is Thine—
    My wealth, my poverty.
Ne'er canst Thou, Lord, resign
    Of Self so much to me:
For, giving Thou hast more;
    But I, henceforth, am poor.

133.

GOD

I see Thee in the distant blue;
But in the violet's dell of dew,
Behold, I *breathe* and *touch* Thee too.

134.

THE SEED

Bearing a life unseen,
Thou lingerest between

A flower withdrawn,
And—what thou ne'er shalt see—
A blossom yet to be
　　When thou art gone.

Unto the feast of spring
Thy broken heart shall bring
　　What most it craved,
To find, like Magdalen
In tears, a life again
　　Love-lost—and saved.

135.　　　　　　SAND

Sterile sister though I be,
Twinborn to the barren sea,
Yet of all things fruitful we
Wait the end; and presently,
Lo, they are not! Then to me
(Children to the nurse's knee)
Come the billows fresh and free,
　　Breathing immortality.

136.　　　　　　BREAD

Still surmounting as I came
Wind and water, frost and flame,
Night and day, the livelong year,
From the burial-place of seed,
From the earth's maternal bosom,
Through the root, and stem, and blossom,
To supply thy present need,
Have I journeyed here.

137.   ON CALVARY

In the shadow of the rood
Love and Shame together stood;
Love, that bade Him bear the blame
Of her fallen sister Shame;
Shame, that by the pangs thereof
Bade Him break His heart for Love.

138.   STILLING THE TEMPEST

'Twas all she could:—The gift that Nature gave,
    The torrent of her tresses, did she spill
Before His feet; and lo, the troubled wave
    Of passion heard His whisper, "Peace, be still!"

139.   ALL IN ALL

We know Thee, each in part—
    A portion small;
But love Thee, as Thou art—
    The All in all:
For Reason and the rays thereof
Are starlight to the noon of Love.

140.   EXALTATION

O leaf upon the highest bough,
The poet of the woods art thou
    To whom alone 'tis given—
The farthest from thy place of birth—
To hold communion with the earth
    Nor lose the light of heaven.

[93]

O leaf upon the topmost height,
Amid thy heritage of light
    Unsheltered by a shade,
'Tis thine the loneliness to know
That leans for sympathy below
    Nor finds what it hath made.

141.   A MEDITATION

'Tis Nothingness that sunders me,
O God, from Thine Eternity,
Wherein, a being yet to be,
I dwelt forever one with Thee,
Till 'twixt Thee and Thy living Thought
This veil of Nothingness was wrought—
A gulf Thy Love alone could span—
The mystery that made me Man.

142.   FAITH

In every seed to breathe the flower,
    In every drop of dew
To reverence a cloistered star
    Within the distant blue;

To wait the promise of the bow,
    Despite the cloud between,
Is Faith—the fervid evidence
    Of loveliness unseen.

143.   HAZARD

One step 'twixt loss and gain!
The summit to attain

So near the brink of pain
　　　Hath joy to go—

So steep the precipice,
So frail the footing is,
'Twere death to panting bliss
　　　To look below.

144.　　　　　THE VAMPIRE MOON

The vital vapors to absorb,
　　　The moon, with famished gaze,
Suspends her lean, malignant orb
　　　Above a dying face.

I watch her like a folded flower
　　　As silently expand;
The pulses waning hour by hour,
　　　And heavier the hand,

Till she hath brimmed her cup, and I
　　　An empty chalice hold;
My heart, in agony, as dry,
　　　In wintriness as cold.

145.　　　　　THE HOUSEHOLDERS

One plucked the grape and trod the wine,
And headlong rushed the sotted swine
　　　To perish in the sea.
One blessed the cup and poured the blood,
And lo! about His banquet stood
　　　The brides of chastity.

146.   SHEET-LIGHTNING

A glance of love or jealousy,
    It flashes to and fro,
A swift sultanic majesty,
    Through Night's seraglio;
Where many a starry favorite
    In reverence profound
Awaits with palpitating light
    A step without a sound.

147.   SLUMBER-SONG

Sleep! the spirits that attend
    On thy waking hours are fled.
Heaven thou canst not now offend
    Till thy slumber-plumes are shed;

Consciousness alone doth lend
    Life its pain, and death its dread;
Innocence and peace befriend
    All the sleeping and the dead.

148.   THE TREE

Planted by the Master's hand
Steadfast in thy place to stand,
While the ever-changing year
Clothes or strips thy branches bare;
Lending not a leaf to hold
Warmth against the winter's cold;
Lightening not a limb the less
For the summer's sultriness;

Nay, thy burden heavier made,
That within thy bending shade
Thankless multitudes, oppressed,
There may lay them down and rest.
Soul, upon thy Calvary
Wait; the Christ will come to thee.

149.   A LEPER'S GRAVE

Here, where untainted flesh hath dread
    Corruption's bride to be,
Her life-long victim finds a bed
    From her embraces free.

150.   ALTER IDEM

'Tis what thou wast—*not* what thou art,
    Which I no longer know—
That made thee sovereign of my heart,
    And serves to keep thee so:

And couldst thou, coming to the throne,
    Thy Self, *unaltered*, see,
Thou mightst the occupant disown
    And scout his sovereignty.

151.   A RUBRIC

The aster puts its purple on
    When flowers begin to fall
To suit the solemn antiphon
    Of Autumn's ritual;

And deigns, unwearied, to stand
In robes pontifical
Till Indian Summer leaves the land,
And Winter spreads the pall.

152.   OCTOBER

Behold, the fleeting swallow
Forsakes the frosty air;
And leaves, alert to follow,
Are falling everywhere,
Like wounded birds, too weak
A distant climb to seek.

And soon, with silent pinions,
The fledglings of the north
From winter's wild dominions
Shall drift affrighted forth,
And, phantom-like, anon
Pursue the phantoms gone.

153.   MEMORY

Lo, the blossom to the bee
Yields not more than thou to me—
Food for love to live upon
When the summer days are gone,
Poorer than they come, to find
What was sweetest, left behind.

154.   CLEOPATRA TO THE ASP

("*Dost thou not see my baby at my breast,*
That sucks the nurse asleep?")

Lie thou where life hath lain,
And let thy swifter pain
        His rival prove;
Till, like the fertile Nile,
Death buries, mile for mile,
        This waste of love.

Soft! Soft! A sweeter kiss
Than Anthony's is this!
        O regal shade,
Luxurious as sleep
Upon thy bosom deep
        My heart is laid.

155.   THE COWSLIP

It brings my mother back to me
Thy frail familiar form to see,
        Which was her homely joy;
And strange that one so weak as thou
Should lift the veil that sunders now
        The mother and the boy.

156.   LEAR'S FOOL

"I'll go to bed at noon."
        Ah, Fool, 'twas wisely said;
For Sorrow ne'er too soon
        The requiem-call to bed.

The Magi came to Bethlehem,
The House of Bread, and following them,
As they the Star, I too am led
To Christ, the living House of Bread.
A pilgrim from the hour of birth,
The night-cold bosom of the earth
I traversed, heavenward journeying,
A hidden prophecy of Spring.
My only guide, a lifted blade
My only weapon, till the Shade,
The latest to withstand me, lay
Death-smitten at the door of Day.
O Light! O heavenly Warmth! to you,
My cup-bearers, I quaffed the dew,
The pledge and sacramental sign
Of Life that, mingling first with mine—
A sap-like inspiration—ran
To mingle with the life of man.
As leaped the Infant in the womb
At Mary's voice, e'en so to bloom
And ripeness, while the reapers sang,
My soul—their songs inspiring—sprang
To meet the scythe, the flail, the stone
Of sacrifice, whereby alone,
Through waves of palpitating flame,
The Bread upon the altar came.
And here, O mystery of Love,
Behold, from highest heaven above,
Through *Me*, the Son of God again,
A victim for the sons of men!

158.   ANONYMOUS

Anonymous—nor needs a name
To tell the secret whence the flame
With light and warmth and incense, came
A new creation to proclaim.

So was it when, His labor done,
God saw His work and smiled thereon:
His glory in the picture shone,
But name upon the canvas none.

159.   THE SONG OF THE MAN

"The woman gave, and I did eat."
         Whereof gave she?
" 'Twas of the garden fruitage sweet—
         A portion fair to see;
She plucked and ate, and I did eat,
         And lost alike are we;
              God saith,
         Ye die the death!"

"The woman gave, and I did eat."
         Whereof gave she?
" 'Twas of her womb a burden sweet—
         But sad, alas, to see;
She took and ate, and I did eat,
         And saved alike are we;
              God saith,
         So dieth death!"

1896

160.   THE MARSH

The woods have voices, and the sea
Her choral-song and threnody;
But thou alike to sun and rain
Dost mute and motionless remain.
As pilgrims to the shrine of sleep,
Through all thy solemn spaces creep
The tides—a moment on thy breast
To pause in sacramental rest;
Then, flooded with the mystery,
To sink reluctant to the sea,
In landward loneliness to yearn
Till to thy bosom they return.

161.   MY SECRET

'Tis not what I am fain to hide
    That doth in deepest darkness dwell,
But what my tongue hath often tried,
    Alas, in vain to tell.

162.   THE DEAD THRUSH

Love of nest and mate and young
Woke the music of his tongue,
While upon the fledgling's brain
Soft it fell as scattered grain,
There to blossom tone for tone
Into echoes of his own.
Doth the passion wholly die
When the fountainhead is dry?
Nay, as vapor from the sea,

Lives the dream eternally;
Soon the silent clouds again
Melt in rhapsodies of rain.

163.   THE YOUNG TENOR

I woke; the harbored melody
        Had crossed the slumber bar,
And out upon the open sea
        Of consciousness afar
Swept onward with a fainter strain,
As echoing the dream again.

So soft the silver sound and clear
        Outpoured upon the night,
That silence seemed a listener
        O'erleaning with delight
The slender moon, a finger-tip
Upon the portal of her lip.

164.   ANTICIPATION

The master scans the woven score
Of subtle harmonies before
        A note is stirred;
And Nature now is pondering
The tidal symphony of Spring,
        As yet unheard.

165.   IN SOLITUDE

Like as a brook that all night long
Sings, as at noon, a bubble-song
        To sleep's unheeding ear,

The poet to himself must sing
When none but God is listening
The lullaby to hear.

166.   PEACH BLOOM

A dream in fragrant silence wrought,
A blossoming of petaled thought,
A passion of these April days—
The blush of nature now betrays.

167.   THE TOLLMEN

Lo, Silence, Sleep, and Death
Await us on the way
To take of each the tribute breath
That God himself did pay.

Nor Solomon's as great
Nor Caesar's strong control,
As his who sits beside his gate
To take of each the toll.

168.   MATER DOLOROSA

Again maternal Autumn grieves,
As blood-like drip the maple leaves
On Nature's Calvary,
And every sap-forsaken limb
Renews the mystery of Him
Who died upon a Tree.

169.   AN APRIL PRAYER
        Lord, to Thy signal-light the trees
            In leaf and flower reply;
        Let not my heart, more dull than these,
            Alone unwakened lie.

170.   FROM PARADISE
        All else that in the limit lies
            Of fleeting time I see;
        The glance, Beloved, of thine eyes
            Alone is lost to me.

        And in the self-same interval,
            The ever-changing place
        Of light's horizon-line is all
            That meets thy lonely gaze.

        Behold the glimmer of a tear,
            The twinkle of a star—
        The shadow and the light how near!
            And yet, alas, how far!

171.   DEUS ABSCONDITUS
        My God has hid Himself from me
        Behind whatever else I see;
        Myself—the nearest mystery—
        As far beyond my grasp as He.

        And yet, in darkest night, I know,
        While lives a doubt-discerning glow,
        That larger lights above it throw
        These shadows in the vale below.

172.

THE BLUEBIRD

When God had made a host of them,
One little flower still lacked a stem
    To hold its blossom blue;
So into it He breathed a song,
And suddenly, with petals strong
    As wings, away it flew.

173.

A REMONSTRANCE

Sing me no more, sweet warbler, for the dart
Of joy is keener than the flash of pain;
Sing me no more, for the re-echoed strain
Together with the silence breaks my heart.

174.

THE SISTERS

    The waves forever move;
    The hills forever rest:
    Yet each the heavens approve,
    And Love alike hath blessed
    A Martha's household care,
    A Mary's cloistered prayer.

175.

RESIGNATION

Behold, in summer's parching thirst,
The while the waters pass them by,
The hills, like Tantalus accurst,
    In silent anguish lie;
Nor look they to the lowly vale
Wherein their famished shadows glide,

But, with uplifted glances pale,
  The will of heaven abide.

176.   THE LOST ANCHOR

Ah, sweet it was to feel the strain,
  What time, unseen, the ship above
  Stood steadfast to the storm that strove
To rend our kindred cords atwain!

To feel, as feel the roots that grow
  In darkness, when the stately tree
  Resists the tempests, that in me
High hope was planted far below!

But now, as when a mother's breast
  Misses the babe, my prisoned power
  Deep-yearning, heart-like, hour by hour,
Unquiet aches in cankering rest.

1897

177.   DESERT-ORBS

The world, they tell us, dwindles
    When matched with other spheres;
And yet in all their amplitudes
    No place for human tears.

How sterile is the sunshine,
    How masculine the blue,
That breeds no shadow, nor betrays
    A memory of dew!

178.   INFLUENCE

He cannot as he came depart—
    The Wind that woos the Rose;
Her fragrance whispers in his heart
    Wherever hence he goes.

179.   NEIGHBOR

Full many a heedless fellow man
    Had passed him on the way,
But Night, the Good Samaritan,
    Beholding where he lay,
Upbore him to the Inn of Sleep,
    And there I heard him say,
"Whate'er the charges of his keep,
    O Landlord, I'll repay."

180.   SOIL-SONG

        I give what ne'er was mine—
            To every seed the power
            Of stem and leaf and flower,
        Of fruit or fragrance fine;

        And take what others loathe—
            Of death the foulest forms,
            Wherewith to feed my worms,
        And thus the world reclothe.

181.   LIFE'S REPETEND

        Do ye forget the blossom-time?
        Or tint for tint, as rhyme for rhyme,
            Would ye, O leaves, supply;
        To prove, as echo to the ear,
        That Near is Far and Far is Near
            In circling home to die?

182.   MEADOW-FROGS

        Ere yet the earliest warbler wakes
            Of coming spring to tell,
        From every marsh a chorus breaks—
            A choir invisible—
        As though the blossoms underground
        A breath of utterance had found.

                    [117]

Whence comes the liquid melody?
    The summer clouds can bring
No fresher music from the sky
    Than here the marshes sing.
Methinks the mists about to rise
Are chanting their rain prophecies.

183.   A SUNSET

What means it, Lord? No Daniel
    In Nature's banquet-hall
Appears, thy messenger, to spell
    The writing on the wall.

Is it the Babylonian doom—
    A kingdom passed away—
A midnight monarch to assume
    The majesty of Day?

1899

184.   BETHEL

A rugged stone
For centuries neglected and alone,
        Its destiny unknown.

The tides of Light
Sped o'er it, and the breakers of the night,
        In alternating flight.

And it was wet
With twilight dew, the sacramental sweat
        That mystic dreams beget.

Here Jacob lay
And saw the midnight vision drift away
        Before the darker day.

Upon the sod
A pillow; then, by countless angels trod,
        A stepping-stone to God.

185.   THE CHILD ON CALVARY

The Cross is tall
And I too small
To reach His hand
Or touch His feet;
But on the sand
His footprints I have found,
And it is sweet
To kiss the holy ground.

AN IDOLATER

The Baby has no skies
But Mother's eyes,
    Nor any God above
    But Mother's Love.
His angel sees the Father's face,
But *he* the Mother's, full of grace;
And yet the heavenly kingdom is
    Of such as this.

1900

187.   TO A STAR

Am I the only child awake
        Beneath thy midnight beams?
If so, for gentle slumber's sake,
        The brighter be their dreams!

But shouldst thou, travelling the deep,
        The silent angel see
That puts the little ones to sleep,
        Bright star, remember me.

188.   AUTUMN

Now at the aged year's decline
Behold the messenger divine
With love's celestial counter-sign,
The sacrament of bread and wine.

189.   ASPIRATION

I envy not the sun
        His lavish light;
But oh, to be the one
        Pale orb of night,
In silence and alone
Communing with mine own!

I envy not the rain
        That freshens all
The parching hill and plain;
        But oh, the small
Night-dewdrop now to be,
My noonday flower, for thee!

190.   A HAIRBREADTH

'Tis in the twinkle of escape
        That all our safety lies.
Of danger, whatsoe'er the shape,
        The nearness naught implies:
This side is life; that side, a breath
        Of deviation, instant death.

'Tis in the *present* I am free
        The mental die to cast;
The future yet of mastery
        Is palsied as the past;
Between, the breathless balance still
        Awaits the hesitating will.

191.   OUTLINES

Oh, frame me in thy love, as I
The landscape in the branches low;
That none beneath the bending sky
        Our sylvan secret know.

For 'tis of life the mystery
That, wheresoe'er its fibres run,
In time or in eternity,
        The many shape the one.

1901

192.   THE ASSUMPTION

Behold! the mother bird
The Fledgling's voice hath heard!
He calls anew,
    "It was thy breast
    That warmed the nest
From whence I flew.
Upon a loftier tree
Of life I wait for thee;
Rise, mother-dove, and come;
Thy Fledgling calls thee home!"

193.   THE BIRTH OF A WORLD

    A hidden world,
    Unwombing, hurled
    From dark to light.
    And to the skies
    Its wondering eyes
    The livelong night
Doth Science turn, with sighs
When shadows take their flight.

    Another birth—
    A soul to earth
    But newly come!
    Its destiny
    Eternity.
    With wonder dumb
The heavens look down to see
Our faces turned therefrom.

[129]

194. **THE OLD PASTOR**

How long, O Lord, to wait
Beside this open gate?
My sheep with many a lamb
Have entered, and I am
Alone, and it is late.

195. **CONSECRATION**

The Twilight to my Star,
    Her hoary head
A Hope receding far,
    To Life re-led.

Apart and poor I lay;
    My fevered frame
Slow withering away,
    When soft she came,

From comfort, to my care;
    And Pity sweet
Subdued her, kneeling there,
    To kiss my feet.

A Magdalen adored
    Her God in Thee:—
A greater love, O Lord,
    Anointed me.

196. **THE RAIN-POOL**

I am too small for winds to mar
My surface; but I hold a Star
That teaches me, though low my lot,
That highest heaven forgets me not.

197.   TO AN AMATEUR
                Love thy violin;
                Let thy soul therein
                Learn the unity
                Of the mystic three,
                When the string and bow—
                Parted lovers—meet
                And in music know
                Life in love complete.

198.   SOOTHSAYERS
        The winds that, gypsy-wise, foretold
                The fortune of today,
        At twilight, with the gathered gold
                Of sunset, stole away;

        And of their cloud accomplices
                That prophesied the rain
        Upon the night-forsaken skies
                No vestiges remain.

199.   THE MIST
        Eurydice eludes the dark
                To follow Orpheus, the lark
        That leads her to the dawn
                With rhapsodies of star-delight,
                Till, looking backward in the flight,
        He finds that she is gone.

                [131]

STABAT MATER

In the shadow of the rood,
Broken-hearted there she stood
 Near her Son and Lord;
While her soul, His doom lamenting,
Yet in sacrifice consenting,
 Felt the cleaving sword.

Thou alone no ransom needing,
Let thy Son, the Victim bleeding,
 For my sin atone;
What for me, my God and Brother
Deigns to bear, O sinless Mother,
 Lean not thou alone.

To the lash, for sin atoning,
Lo, He bows! and thou, O moaning
 Mother, now must see
Limb from limb His spirit languish,
And His latest looks of anguish,
 Turned in love to thee!

Came there ever to another
Grief like thine, O wounded Mother,
 As thou lookest upon
Him, the son of God, all holy,
And of thee, a virgin lowly,
 Sole-begotten Son?

Who so lost to human feeling
As to hide his tears revealing
 Sympathy with thine?
Who that e'er was born of woman,

In a tenderness so human,
　　Sees not love divine?

Let me near the fountain growing
Of thy tenderness o'erflowing,
　　Drink my fill thereof;
Let the fervid flames illuming
All thy soul, a fire consuming,
　　Kindle mine to love.

One with thee, my vigil keeping;
One with thee, the mourner, weeping
　　Near His sacred side,
Where thy soul in desolation
Waits of woe the consummation,
　　Let my soul abide.

Virgin, earth's divinest blossom,
Spurn not from thy fragrant bosom
　　Dews that fall for thee!
Make me, near thy son remaining,
Simon-like, His cross sustaining
　　One in sympathy!

Let me from His life-distilling
Wounds, mine empty chalice filling,
　　Quaff the crimson wine;
Let the flames, devouring, end me,
In thy chastity defend me
　　From the wrath divine.

Lord, through her who brought Thee hither,
Let me, hence departing whither

Thou the way hast found,
Come through Death's opposing portal
To the Victor's palm immortal,
With Thy glory crowned.

201.   BARGAINS

"What have you in your basket?"
I questioned Mother Sleep.
"Ah, many a golden casket
Of jewel-dreams I keep
At pastime prices for the friend
Who has half-an-hour or more to spend."

202.   "CHANTICLEER"

A crowing, cuddling little Babe was he,
A child for little children far or near.
When he stood and crowed upon his mother's knee,
The morning echoed, "Welcome, Chanticleer!"
He was a crowing, cuddling little Babe!

When his mother wore, alas, her life away,
He was wonder wide to see the children weep,
But he crowed, and cuddled close enough to lay
His head upon her heart, and went to sleep:—
He was a cuddling, crowing little Babe!

God Himself was tender to him; for, behold,
An Angel in a dream (the children said)

Came and kissed him till his little cheek was cold;
So he never saw the tears the Twilight shed.
He was a crowing, cuddling little Babe!

203.   THE CHRIST CHILD TO THE
            CHRISTMAS LAMB

O little lamb,
Behold I am
So weak and small
That even thou
Canst pity now
The God of all.

204.   THE WHIP-POOR-WILL

From yonder wooded hill
I hear the whip-poor-will,
      Whose mate or wandering echo answers him
      Athwart the lowlands dim.

He calls not through the day;
But when the shadows gray
      Across the sunset draw their lengthening veil,
      He tells his twilight tale.

What unforgotten wrong
Haunts the ill-omened song?
      What scourge of fate has left its loathed mark
      Upon the cringing dark?

[135]

"Whip! Whip-poor-will!"
O sobbing voice, be still!
    Tell not again, O melancholy bird,
    The legend thou hast heard!

205.   WOOD-GRAIN

This is the way that the sap-river ran
From the root to the top of the tree—
    Silent and dark,
    Under the bark,
Working a wonderful plan
    That the leaves never know,
    And the branches that grow
On the brink of the tide never see.

1902

206.   CONSCIENCE

I am that Tamerlane,
        The Scourge of God;
With me alone remain
        The sword and rod
Wherewith in wrath throughout His world-domain,
        Doth Love, avenging, reign.

I am that Joseph bound
        And sold in vain;
From dungeon darkness found
        To rise again;
At God's right hand, whate'er of good redound,
        His sole vicegerent crowned.

207.   MY CAPTIVE

I brought a blossom home with me
        Beneath my roof to stay;
But timorous and frail was she,
        And died before the day:
She missed the measureless expanse
Of heaven, and heaven her countenance.

208.   BETRAYAL

"Whom I shall kiss," I heard a Sunbeam say,
        "Take him and lead away!"
Then, with the Traitor's salutation, "Hail!"
        He kissed the Dawn-Star pale.

209.   THE SHELL

Silence—a deeper sea—
Now sunders thee
Save from the primal tone—
Thy mother's moan.

Within her waves, hadst thou
No voice as now;
A life of exile long
Hath taught thee song.

210.   LEAF AND SOUL
                        Leaf
Let go the Limb?
My life in him
        Alone is found.
Come night, come day,
'Tis here I stay
        Above the sapless ground.

                        Soul
Let go the warm
Lip-kindled form
        And upward fly?
Come joy, come pain,
I here remain,
        Despite the yearning sky.

A sudden frost—and lo!
Both Leaf and Soul let go.

211. **FOG**

The ghost am I
Of winds that die
    Alike on land or sea,
In silence deep
To shroud and keep
    Their mournful memory.

A spirit white,
I stalk the night,
    Or, shadowing the skies,
Forbid the sun
To look upon
    My noonday mysteries.

212. **THE TRUANT**

Listen! 'tis the Rain
Coming home again;
Not as when he went away,
Silent, but in tears to say
    He is sorry to have gone
With the Mist that lured him on;
    And he promises anew
    Nevermore the like to do.
Alas! no sooner shines the sun
Than the selfsame deed is done.

213. **TO HER FIRST-BORN**

Long I waited, wondering
    How, so near my heart,
Love another life could bring,
    Made of mine a part,

Nor let me, save in fancy, gaze
Soul-centered, on thy cloistered face!

But now, the mystery removed,
 Thou liest on my breast,
A form so fervently beloved,
 So tenderly caressed,
That as my spirit compassed thine,
Thy soul the limit seems of mine.

So, life that vanishes anon,
 Perchance about us lies,
Too near for Love to look upon
 With unanointed eyes,
Till, past the interval of pain,
We clasp the living form again.

214.   CONSUMMATION
  The interval
  We both recall,
  To each was all.

  A moment's space,
  That time nor place
  Can e'er efface.

  'Tis all our own,
  A secret known
  To us alone:

  My life to thee
  As thine to me,
  Eternity.

1903

215.   NOCHE TRISTE

That night that bore me to my dead,
    Along the dreary way
The meadow-frogs in chorus said,
    "We sing the vanished day;
Think not that life is all with you:
Her night hath stars and voices too."

216.   WRINKLES

This, biting Frost—this, branding Sun—
This, Wind or drenching Rain hath done;
Each perfecting the Sculptor's plan
    Upon the godlike image, Man.

217.   HELPLESSNESS

In patience as in labor must thou be
    A follower of Me,
Whose hands and feet, when most I wrought for thee,
    Were nailed unto a tree.

218.   RACERS

The winds from many a cloudy mane
Shake off the sweat of gathering rain
    And whicker with delight;
No slope of pasture-lands they need,
Whereon to rest or drink or feed,
Their life the rapture of the speed,
    The frenzy of the flight.

[145]

CHORISTERS

O wind and waters, ye alone
Have chanted the primeval tone
    Since Nature first began.
All other voices change, but ye
Abide, the soul of harmony
    Interpreting the man.

He listens, and his heart is fain
To fashion an immortal strain;
    Yet his sublimest lay
Is but the music of a tongue
Attuned to silence, and among
    The echoes dies away.

1904

220.   THE HAUNTED MOON

Still closer doth she cowl with night
            Her visage white,
To hide her from the spectre gray
            Of yesterday,
Deep buried in his sepulchre
            To all but her.

221.   OUR FIRST BORN

It died so young! and yet,
            Of all that vanished hence,
Is none to lingering regret
            So lost as Innocence:

For wheresoe'er we go,
            Whatever else remain,
That Favorite of Heaven, we know,
            We shall not find again.

222.   TRIUMPH

Despite the North Wind's boast,
            Despite the muffled host
                Of hushing Snow,
            There cometh from below
Out of the darkness wakened, one by one,
            The dreamers of the Sun—
                Not in the bleak array
Of Winter, but with fragrant banners gay
            Leaping the barriers strong
            Of Ice, and loosing Song,
            The prisoner, and letting go

Long-fettered Laughter, as the shadowy Foe
Shrinks from the echoing cry
Of "Life and Victory!"

223.   POE'S PURGATORY

All others rest; but I
Dream-haunted lie—
A distant roar,
As of tumultuous waters, evermore
About my brain.

E'en sleep, though fain
To soothe me, flies affrighted, and alone
I bear the incumbent stone
Of death
That stifles breath,
But not the hideous chorus crying "Shame!"
Upon my name.

Had I not Song?
Yea, and it lingers yet
The souls to fret
Of an ignoble throng,
Aflame with hate
Of the exulting fate
That hurls her idols from her temple fair
And shrines me there.

224.   CHRIST AND THE PAGAN

I had no God but these,
The sacerdotal trees,
And they uplifted me.
"I hung upon a Tree."

The sun and moon I saw,
And reverential awe
Subdued me day and night.
"I am the perfect Light."

Within a lifeless stone—
All other gods unknown—
I sought Divinity.
"The Corner-Stone am I."

For sacrificial feast
I slaughtered man and beast,
Red recompense to gain.
"So I, a Lamb, was slain.

*"Yea, such My hungering Grace
That, wheresoe'er My face
Is hidden, none may grope
Beyond eternal Hope."*

225.   WINTER RAIN

Rain on the roof and rain
On the burial-place of grain;
To one a voice in vain;
To one o'er hill and plain
The pledge of life again.

Rain on the sterile sea,
That hath no need of thee,
Nor keeps thy memory—
'Tis thou that teachest me
The range of charity.

226.   FINIS

O to be with thee sinking to thy rest,
    Thy journey done;
The world thou leavest blessing thee and blest,
    O setting sun;
The clouds, that ne'er the morning joys forget,
    Again aglow,
And leaf and flower with tears of twilight wet
    To see thee go.

227.   MY ANGEL

O little child, that once was I
    And still in part must be,
When other children pass me by,
    Again thy face I see.

Where art thou? Can the Innocence
    That here no more remains,
Forget, though early banished hence,
    What Memory retains?

Alas! and could'st thou look upon
    The features that were thine,
To see of tender graces none
    Abiding now in mine,

Thy heart compassionate would plead,
  And, haply, not in vain,
As Angel Guardian, home to lead
  The wanderer again.

228.   DEJECTION

The sun is gone; and the forsaken sea—
  Her glance a tear
Wherein all depths of tenderness appear—
  Looks back at me,
Where I upon the strand,
The center of the lone horizon, stand
  Forlorn as she,
To know that when her darkness drifts away,
  My own must stay.

229.   IN ÆTERNUM

If Life and Death be things that seem,
If Death be sleep, and Life a dream,
May not the everlasting sleep
The dream of Life eternal keep?

1906

230.   INITIATED

Thou hast put on the livery,
        And learned the shibboleth,
And pledged for all eternity
        The brotherhood of death.

Yet to thy wonder-wakened eyes
        The light, however clear,
But solves the deeper mysteries
        That lay about thee here.

231.   BROTHER ASS AND ST. FRANCIS

It came to pass
That "Brother Ass"
(As he his Body named)
Unto the Saint
Thus made complaint:
"I am unjustly blamed.

"Whate'er I do,
Like Balaam you
Requite me with a blow,
As for offence
To recompense
An ignominious foe.

"God made us one,
And I have done
No wickedness alone;
Nor can I do
Apart, as you,
An evil all my own.

[159]

"If Passion stir,
'Tis you that spur
My frenzy to the goal;
Then be the blame
Where sits the shame,
Upon the goading soul.

"Should one or both
Be blind or loth
Our brotherhood to see,
Remember this,
You needs must miss
Or enter heaven through *me*."

To this complaint
The lowly Saint
In tears replied, "Alas,
If so it be,
God punish me
And bless thee, Brother Ass."

232.   THE CLIFFS
Forever face to face,
As towered of old
Within the Holy Place
The wings of gold.

One heralding the day
With kindled crest;
One reddened with the ray
That fires the west.

[160]

The bosom-vale between
Alike to their own;
To each a heaven unseen,
A world unknown.

1907

233.   THE GRAVE-DIGGER

Here underneath the sod,
    Where night till now hath been,
With every lifted clod
    I let the sunshine in.

How dark soe'er the gloom
    Of death's approaching shade,
The first within the tomb
    Is light, that cannot fade.

And from the deepest grave
    I banish it in vain;
For, like a tidal wave,
    Anon 'twill come again.

234.   ANIMULA VAGA

A spirit from the grave
    Again I come,
E'en as I vanished, save
    Disrobed and dumb.

No shadow as I pass—
    However clear
The wave on mirroring glass—
    Betrays me near;

Nor unto them that live
    Forlorn of me,
A signal can I give
    Of sympathy.

[165]

Ah, better 'twere to hide
  Where none appear
Than thus in death abide
  To life so near!

235.   A SUNSET SONG

Fade not yet, O summer day,
For my love hath answered yea;
Keep us from the coming night,
Lest our blossom suffer blight.

Fear thou not; if love be true,
Closer will it cleave to you.
'Tis the darkened hours that prove
Faith or faithlessness in love.

1908

236.   GOING BLIND

Back to the primal gloom
    Where life began,
As to my mother's womb
    Must I a man
        Return:
Not to be born again,
    But to remain;
And in the School of Darkness learn
    What mean
"The things unseen."

237.   IN BLINDNESS

For me her life to consecrate,
    My Lady Light
Within her shadowy convent gate
    Is lost to sight.
I may not greet her; but a grace—
    A gleam divine—
The rapture of her hidden face
    Suffuses mine.

238.   HER PILOT

Death seemed afraid to wake her;
    For, traversing the deep,
When home he came to take her,
    He kept her fast asleep.

And, haply, from her dreaming
    Of many a risk to run

She woke, with rapture beaming,
To find her voyage done.

239.　　　　　THE IMAGE-MAKER

"Thou shalt no graven image make";
And yet, O sculptor, for the sake
　　　Of such an effigy as I—
The superscription like the face
Disfigured now, and hard to trace,
　　　Didst thou thyself consent to die.

240.　　　　　WAVES

We sighed of old till underneath His feet
　　　Our pulses beat,
Again to sigh in restlessness until
　　　He saith, "Be still."

And with us is the ever-moving wind,
　　　And all mankind—
A triple chorus—each upheaving breast,
　　　A sigh for rest.

241.　　　　　BLIND

Again as in the desert way,
Behold my guides, a cloud by day,
　　　A flame by night;
For darkness wakens with the morn,
But dreams, of midnight slumber born,
　　　Bring back the light.

242.   TIDES

             Like inland streams, O sea,
                 Through joy and pain
             All nature dreams of thee;
                 Nor more appears
             Thy life in mist or rain
                 Than in our tears.

243.   THE SMITER

     They bound Thine eyes and questioned, "Tell us now
     Who smote Thee." Thou wast silent. When today
     Mine eyes are holden, and again they say,
     "Who smote thee?" Lord, I tell them it is Thou.

244.   MY PORTION

             I know not what a day may bring;
             For now 'tis sorrow that I sing
                 And now 'tis joy.
             In both a father's hand I see;
             For one renews the man in me,
                 And one the boy.

245.   IMPORT

             Thou hast the final touch supplied
             That till thy coming was denied—
             A single letter in a word
             Whose absence all the context blurred;
             A missing note that, but for thee,
             Had marred the perfect harmony.

                      [173]

246.   SURVIVAL
                   The tempest past—
                   A home in ruin laid;
                   But lo! where last
                   The little children played
                   At hide-and-seek,
                   A footprint small
                   Pleads silently,
                   As if afraid to speak.
                   "Behold in me
                   A memory,
                   The least and last of all!"

247.   MAMMY
               I loved her countenance whereon,
                   Despite the longest day,
               The tenderness of visions gone
                   In shadow seemed to stay.
               And now, when faithless sight is fled
                   Beyond my waking gaze,
               Of darkness I am not afraid—
                   It is my Mammy's face.

248.   FIAT LUX
         "Give us this day our daily bread," and *light*;
               For more to me, O Lord, than food is sight:
                   And I at noon have been
             In twilight, where my fellow-men were seen
                   "As trees" that walked before me. E'en today

From time to time there falls upon my way
    A feather of the darkness. But again
It passes; and amid the falling rain
    Of tears, I lift, O Lord, mine eyes to Thee,
        For, lo! I *see!*

THE ROSARY
IN RHYME

249.   **THE ANNUNCIATION**

Accustomed in the highest heights to be,
The Angel bowed in awe,
As if, amazed before Humility,
A deeper heaven he saw.

250.   **THE VISITATION**

His cloistered God the unborn messenger
Exulting, leaped to hear:
His mother in the Mother of her Lord
Interpreting the Word.

251.   **THE NATIVITY**

(*"Born during High Mass"*)
So small that lesser lowliness
Must bow to worship or caress:
So great that heaven itself to know
Love's majesty must look below.

252.   **THE PRESENTATION**

Where, woman, is thine offering—
The debt of law and love?
"My Babe a tender nestling is,
And I the Mother-dove."

253.   **THE CHILD IN THE TEMPLE**

Among the sages while He sat,
And they delighted heard,
None knew the Child they wondered at,
Was God's Eternal Word.

[179]

254.   THE AGONY

Here, where with bloody sweat
The ground is wet,
The brutal thorn is bred
To crown His head:—
Dost thou, avenging sod,
Curse home thy God?

255.   THE CROWN OF THORNS

Oh, wherefore were we torn,
Reluctant from the bough,
To be a mark of scorn
Upon this bleeding Brow?
O fruit of the Forbidden Tree,
Behold the ripened penalty!

256.   THE SCOURGING

O Thongs, for thirst
Of fiends accurst,
Ye quaffed the crimson flood!
Ah, would that we
Who wound, as ye
Were guiltless of His blood!

257.   CARRYING THE CROSS

When Christ went up to Calvary,
His load upon Him laid,

Each tree unto its neighbor tree
In awful silence said,
"Behold, the Gardener is He
Of Eden and Gethsemane!"

258.   THE CRUCIFIXION

Why, O my God, hast Thou forsaken me?
Not so my Mother; for behold and see
She steadfast stands. O Father, shall it be
That she abides when Thou forsakest me?

The Glorious Mysteries

259.   THE RESURRECTION

Behold, the night of sorrow gone,
Like Magdalene the tender Dawn
Goes forth with love's anointing sweet,
To kiss again the Master's feet.

260.   THE ASCENSION

On Sinai did the cloud,
His glory shroud;
And in the Holy Place
It hid His face.
As now He goes, so shall ye see
Him come;—a cloud His canopy.

261.   PENTECOST

Discord—the curse of Babel—done,
The world, divided, hears as one
All hearts revealing each to each,
The new-found harmony of speech.

[181]

262.   THE ASSUMPTION

(*"Preached in Richmond, August 1893"*)

Nor Bethlehem nor Nazareth
Apart from Mary's care,
Nor heaven itself a home for Him
Were not His Mother there.

263.   THE CORONATION OF MARY

Thee, Mother-Queen of Heaven, He crowned,
And not for love alone;
For in thy bosom first He found
The life-spring of His own.

INDEX

Italic print indicates titles, roman indicates first lines of the poems. The numeral refers to the number assigned to the poem in this collection.

[183]

[185]

[189]

A NOTE ON THE TYPE

IN WHICH THIS BOOK WAS SET

This book has been set in Electra, a type face created in
1935 by W. A. Dwiggins, the well-known Boston artist.
This type falls within the "modern" family of type
styles, but was drawn to avoid extreme contrast between
"thick and thin" elements that marks most "modern"
types faces. The design is not based upon any traditional
model, and is not an attempt to revive or to reconstruct
any historic type. Since its birth, Electra has met with
success because of its easy-to-read quality. This book was
composed and printed by the York Composition Company, Inc., of York, and bound by Moore and Company
of Baltimore. The design and typography of this book
are by Howard N. King.